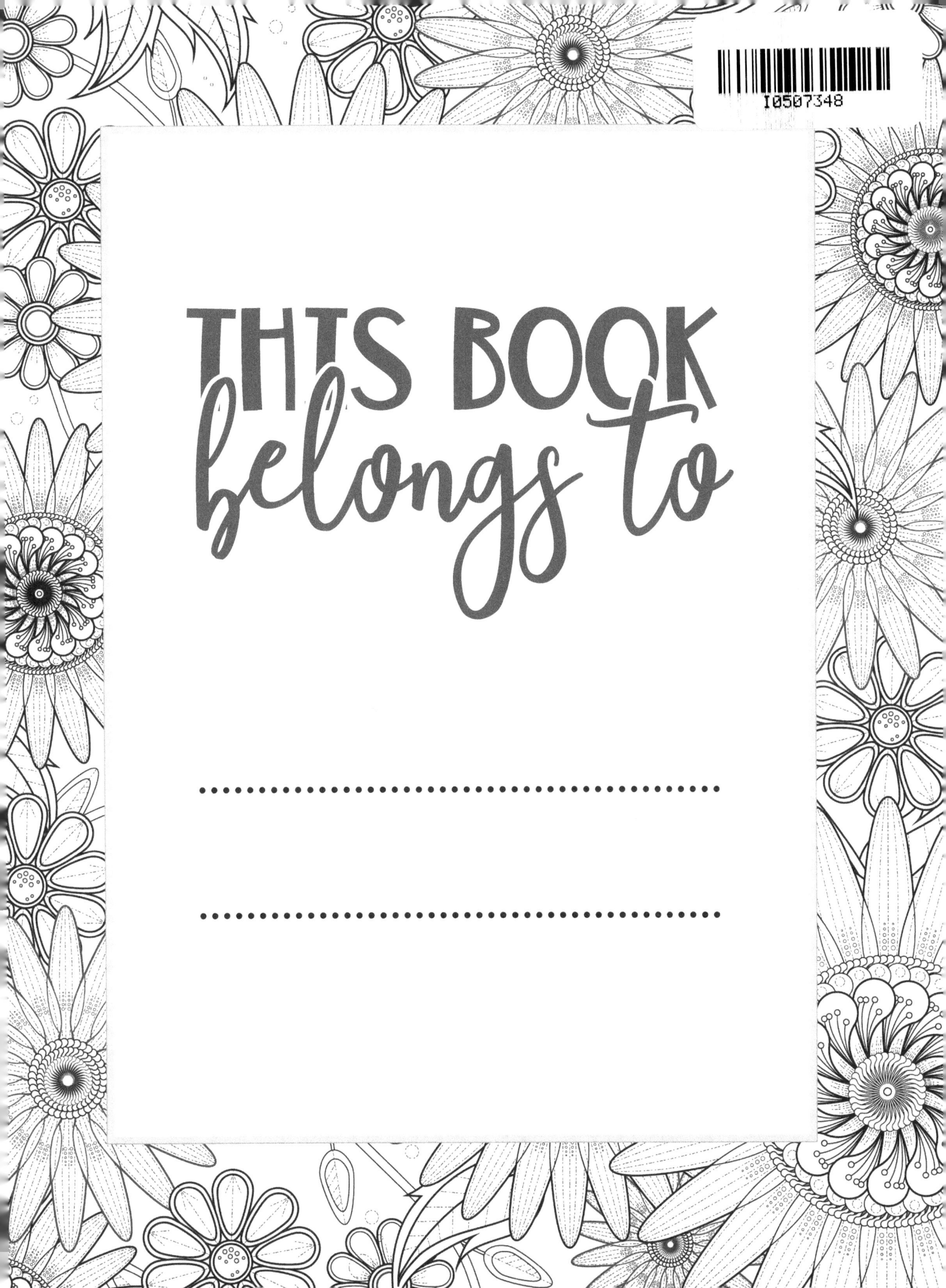

Copyright © 2021 City4moms Publishing
all right reserved

No part of this book may be reproduced, transmitted, or stored in any form or by any means except for your own personal use or for a book review, without the express written permission of the author.

city4momspublishing@gmail.com

for more information on our books please visit

www.city4moms-publishing.com

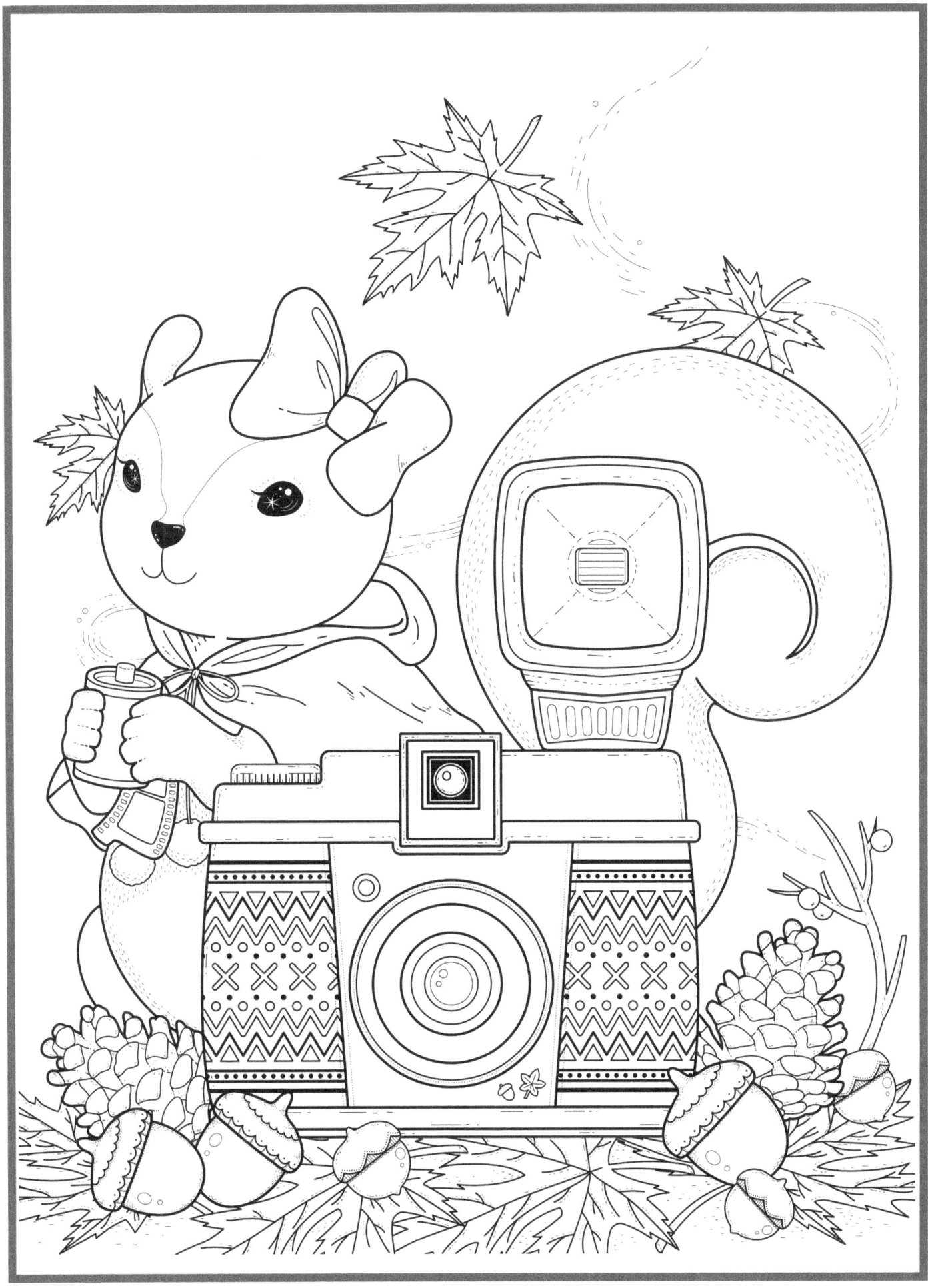

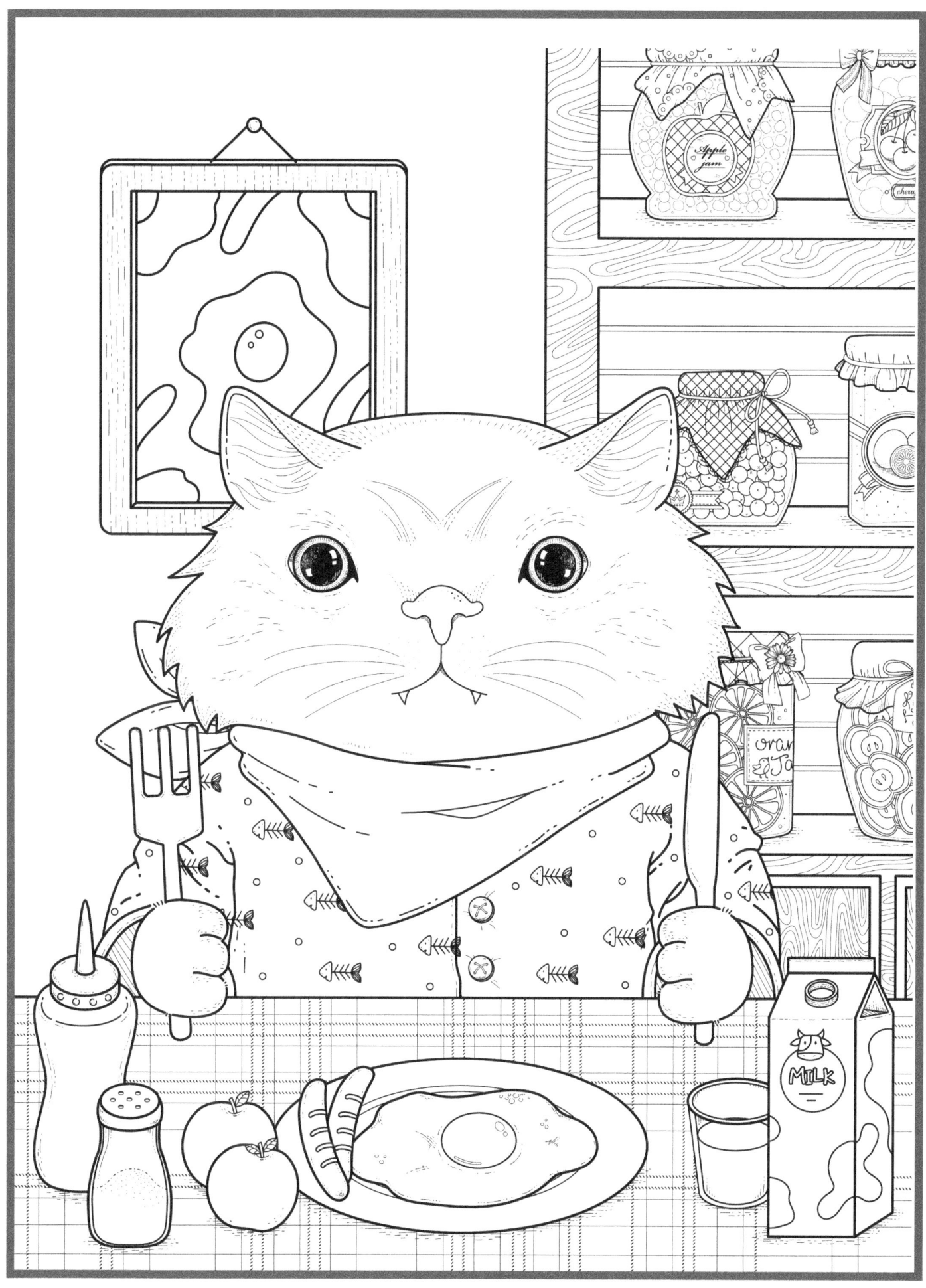

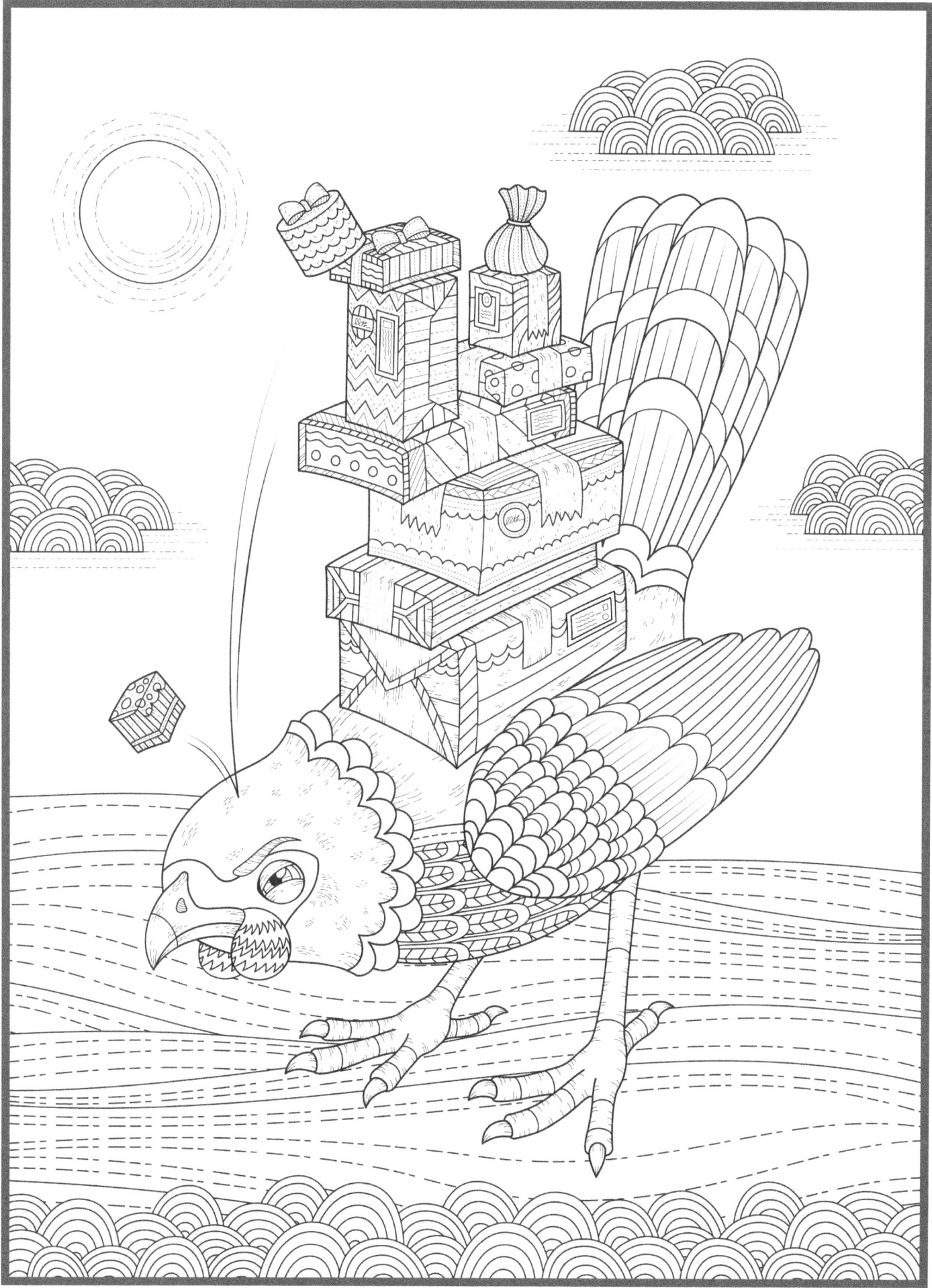

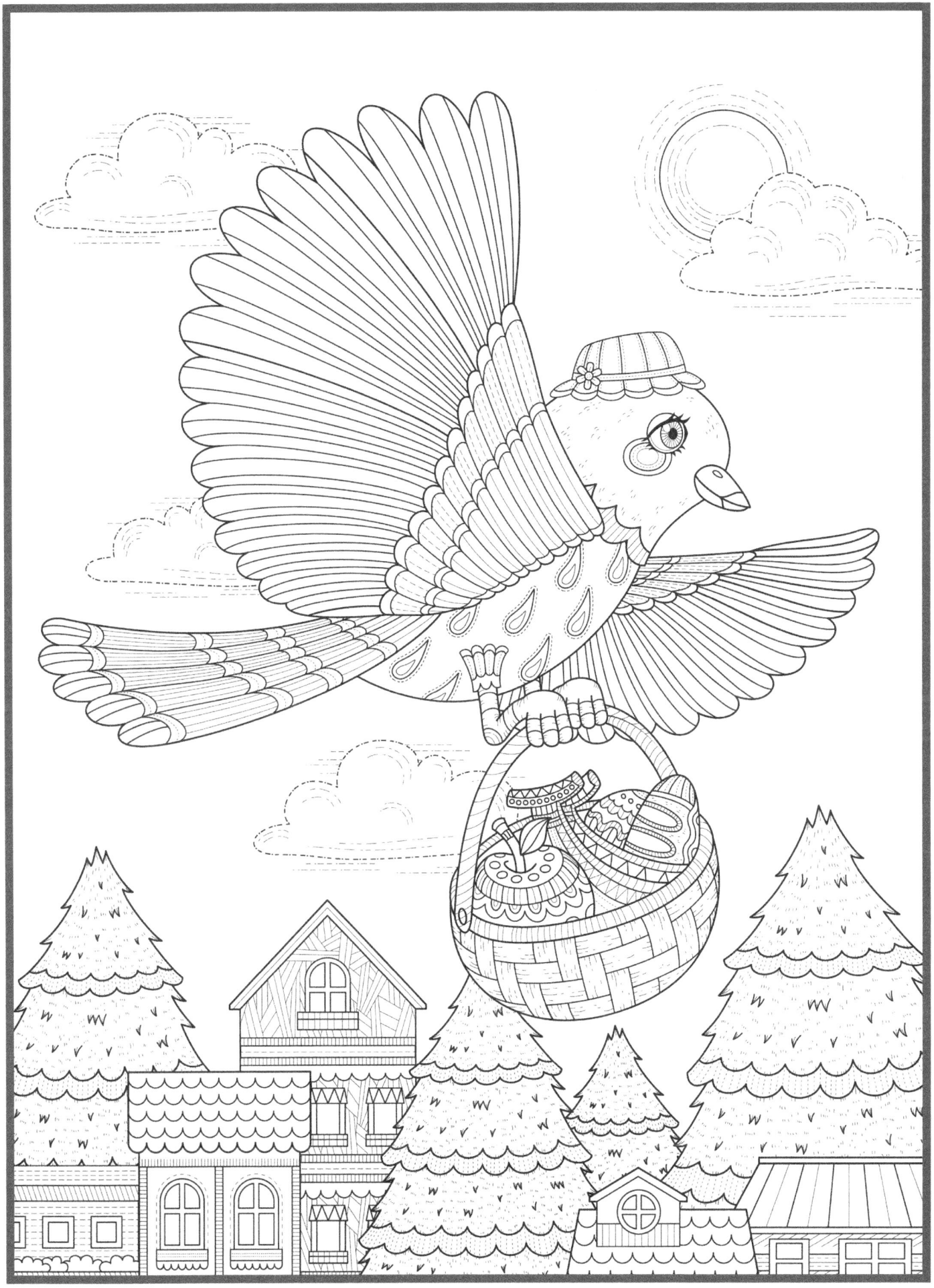

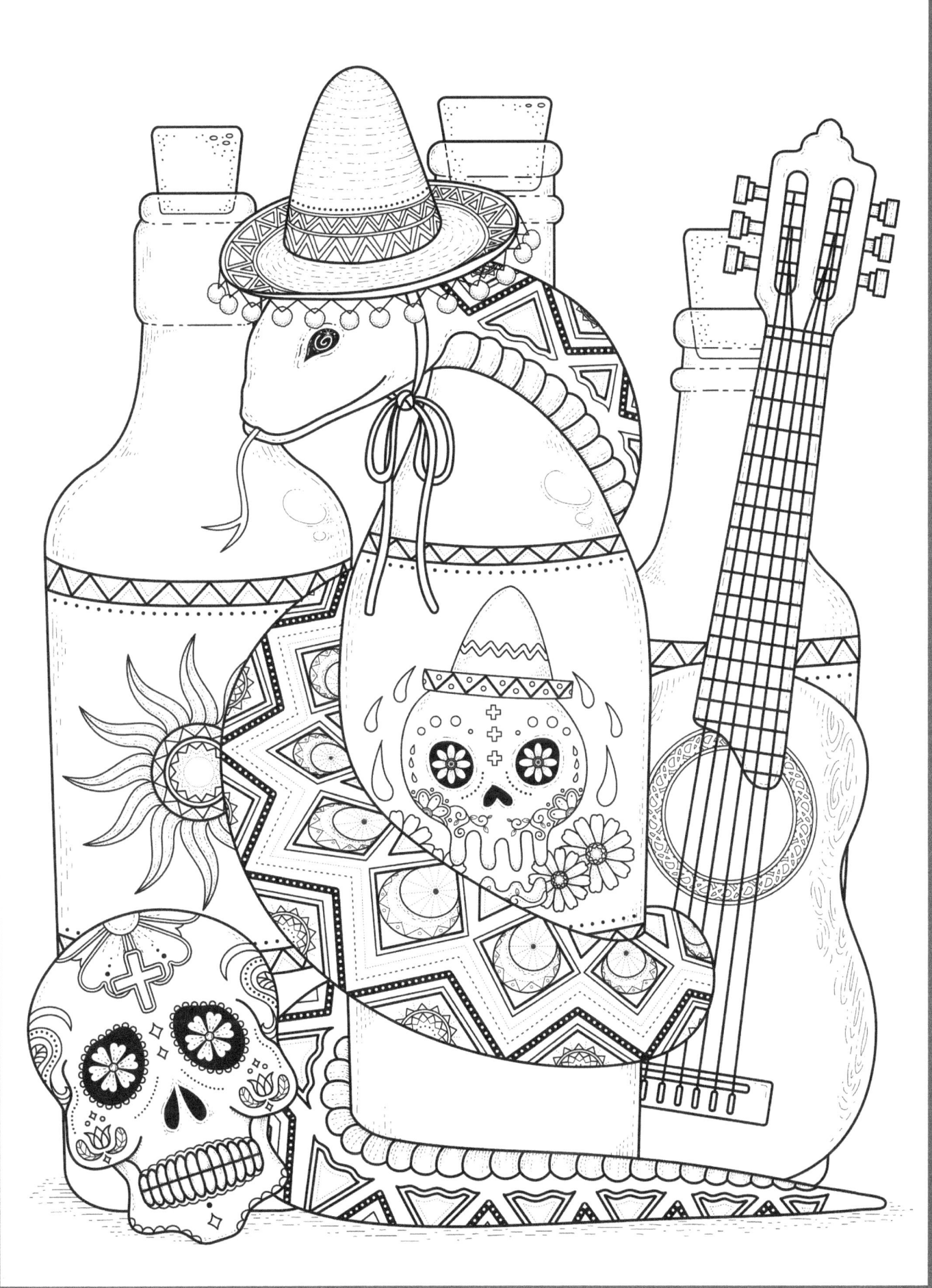

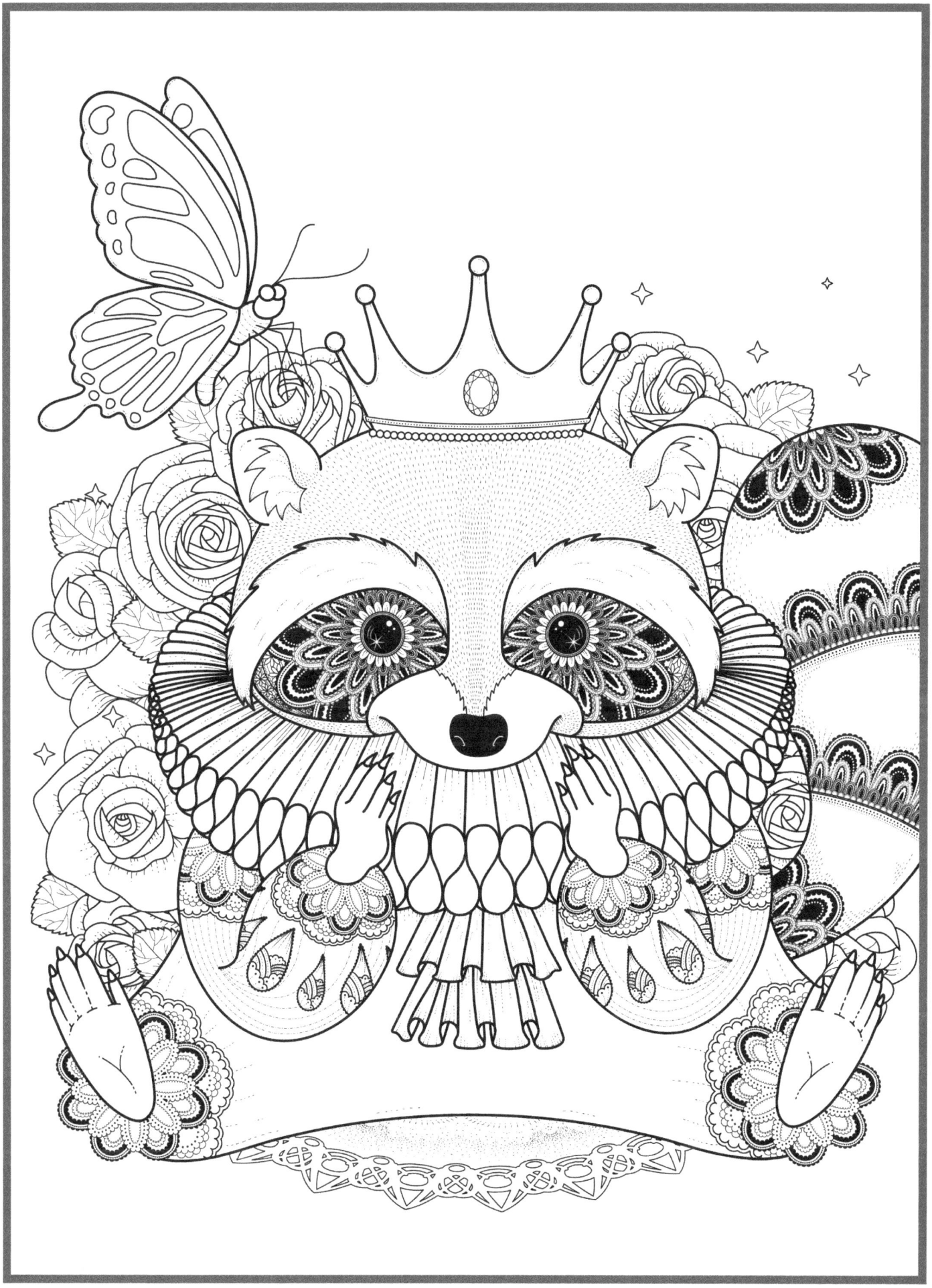

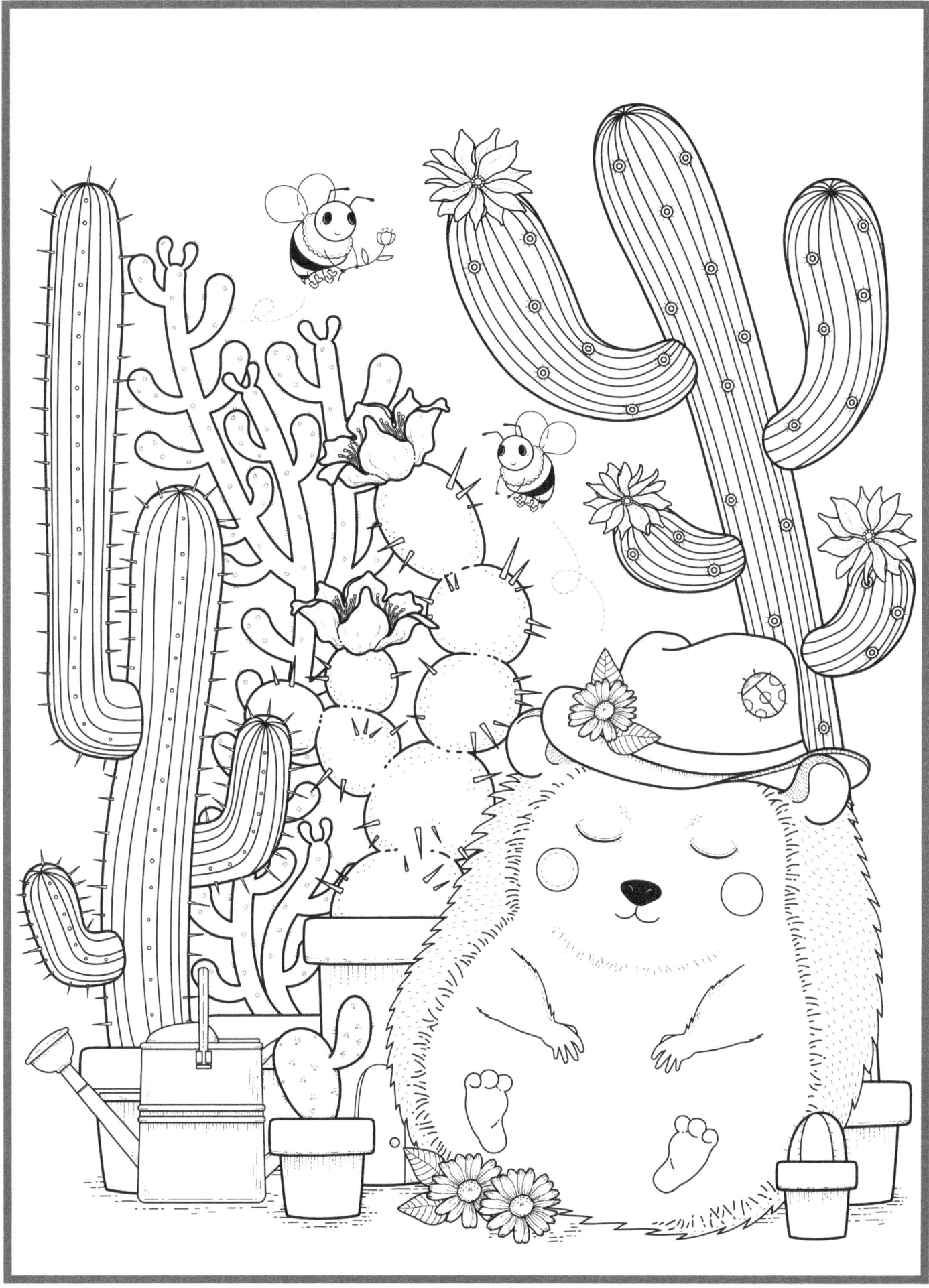

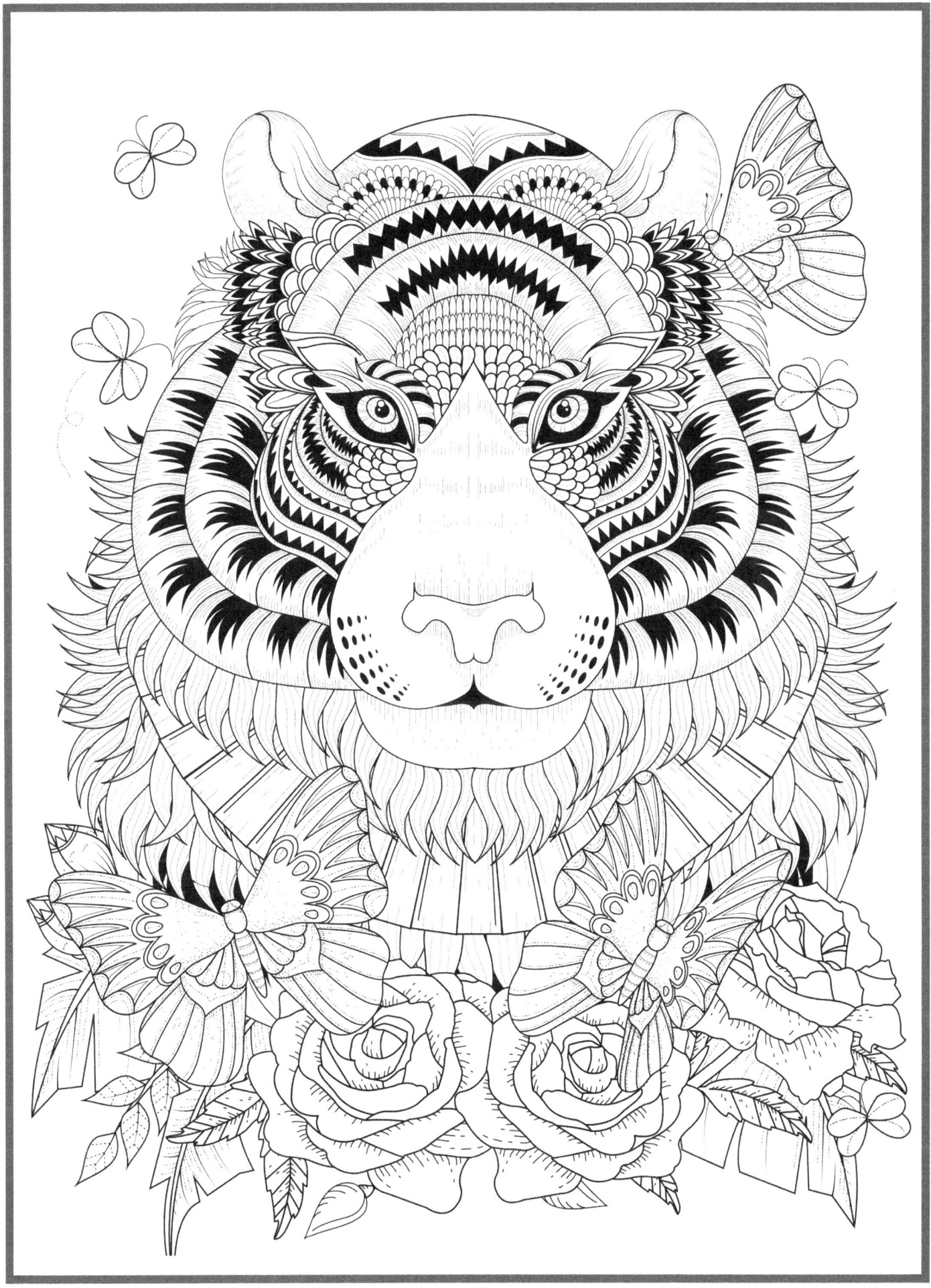

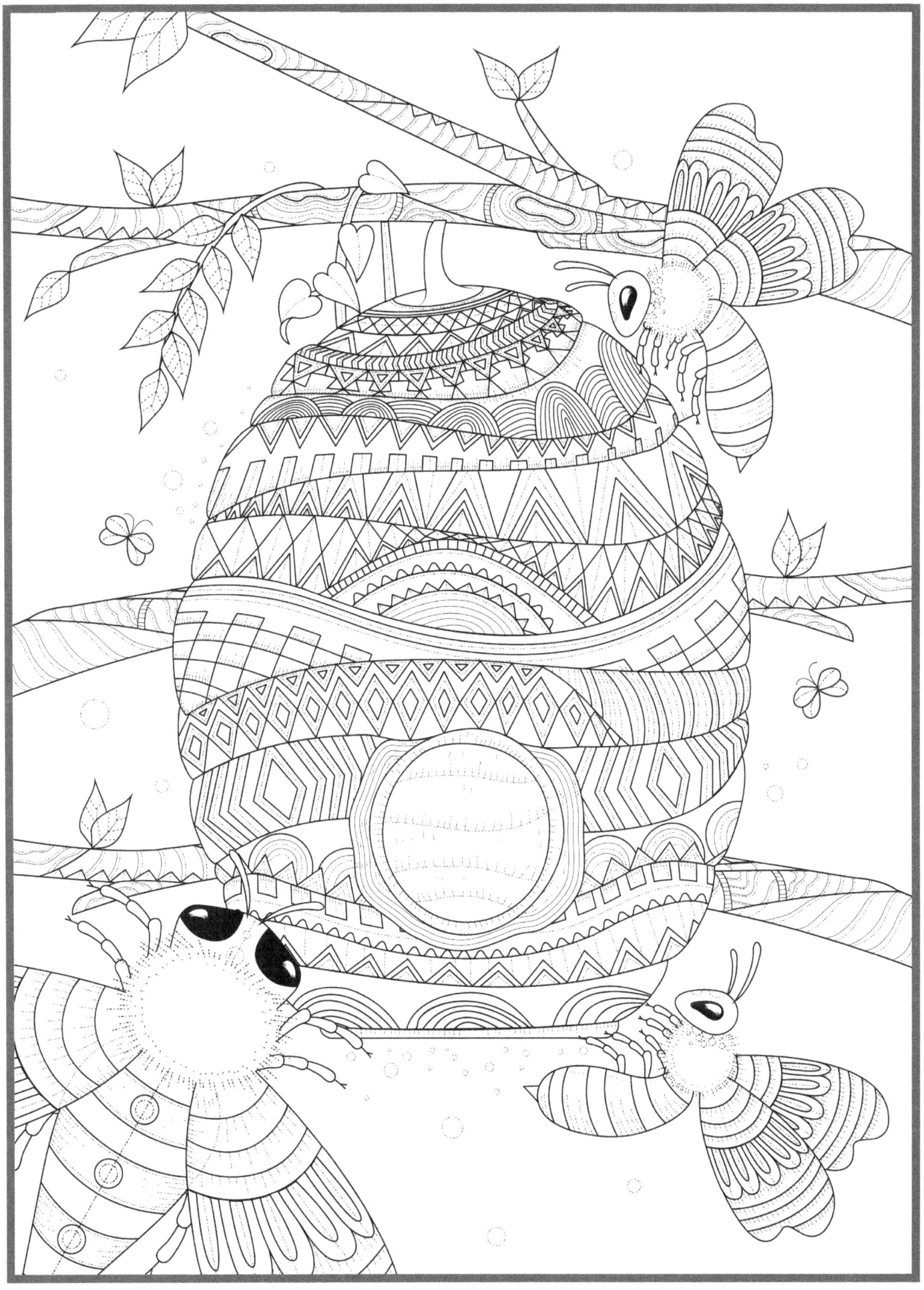

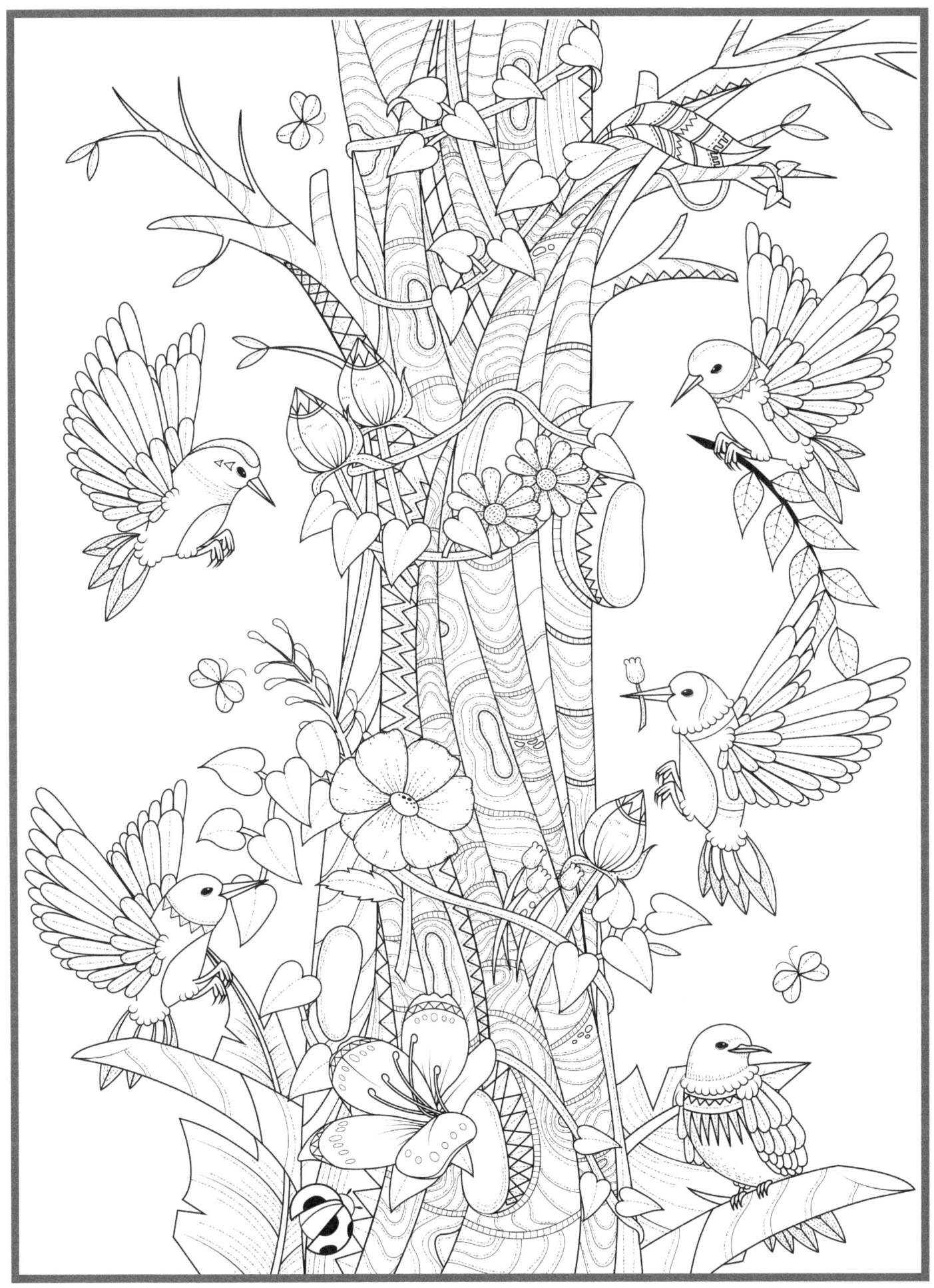

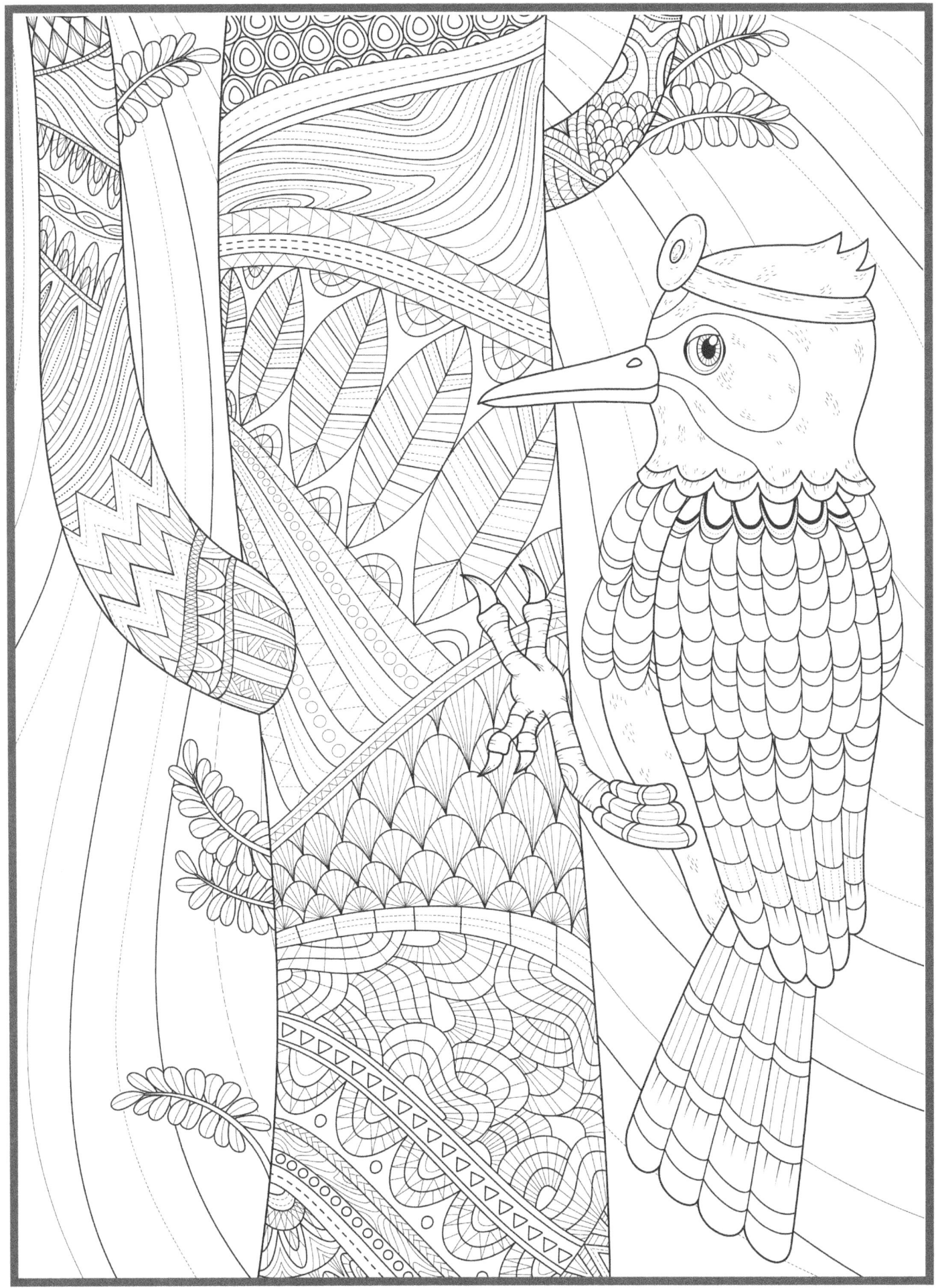

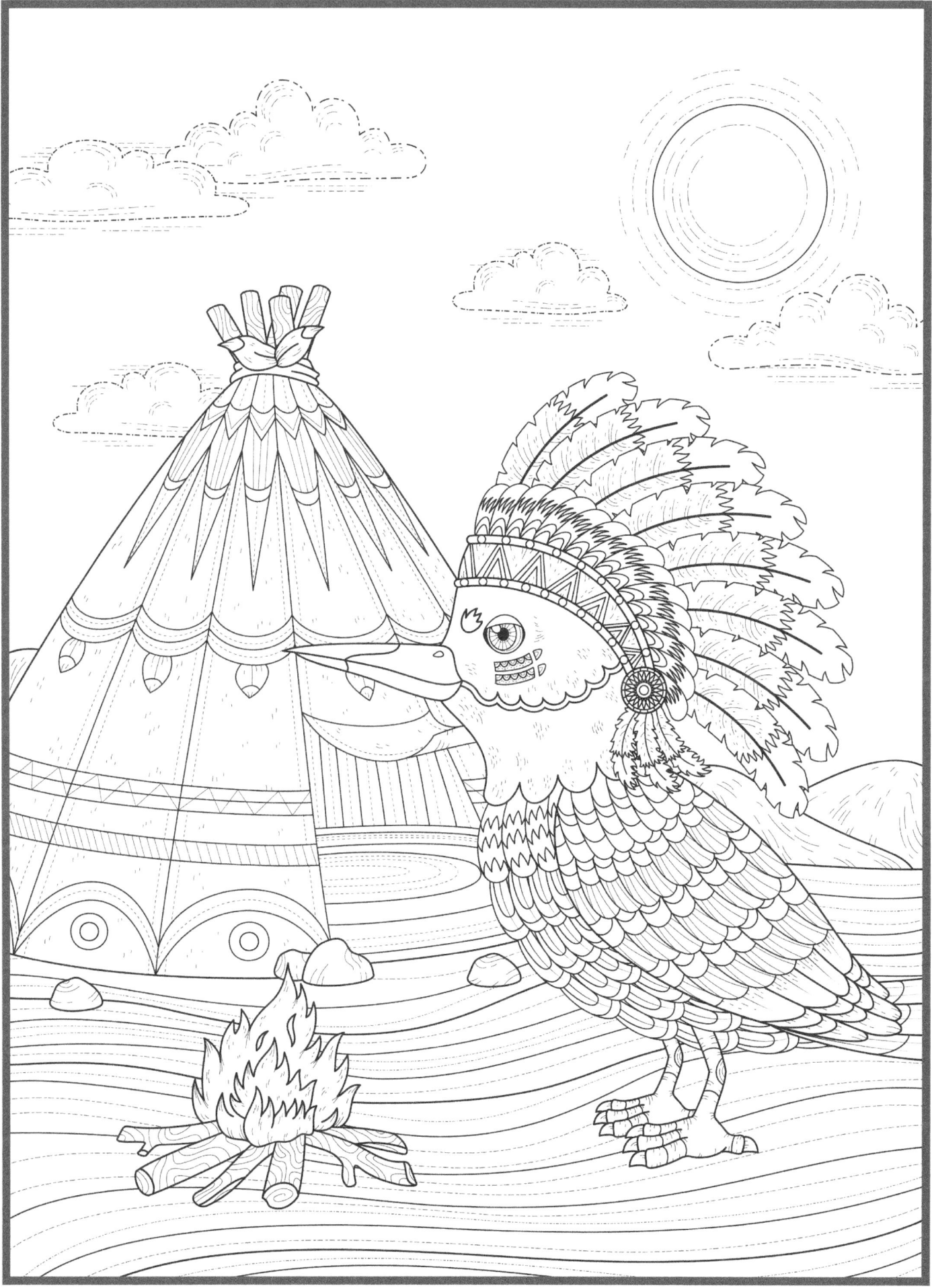

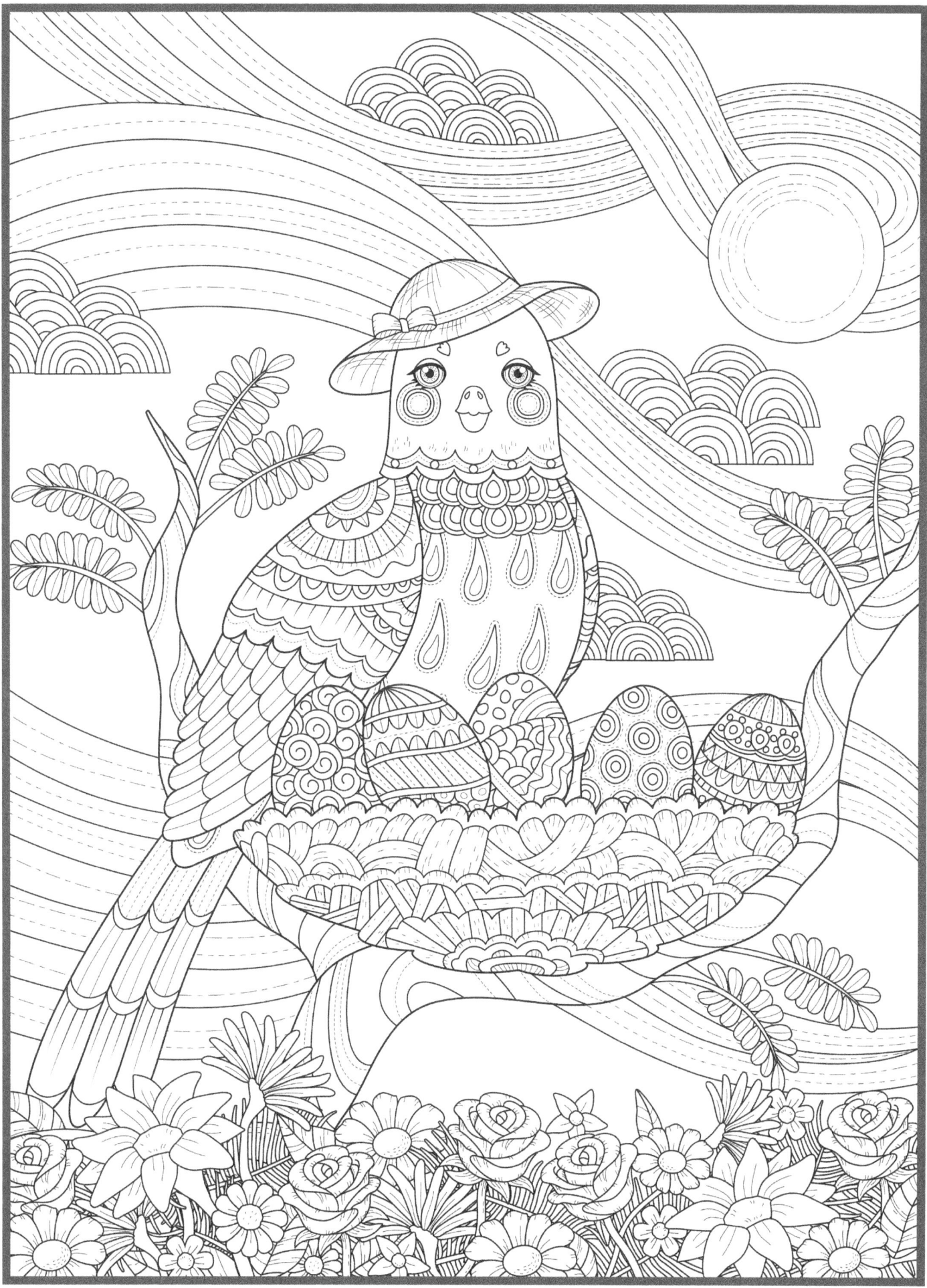

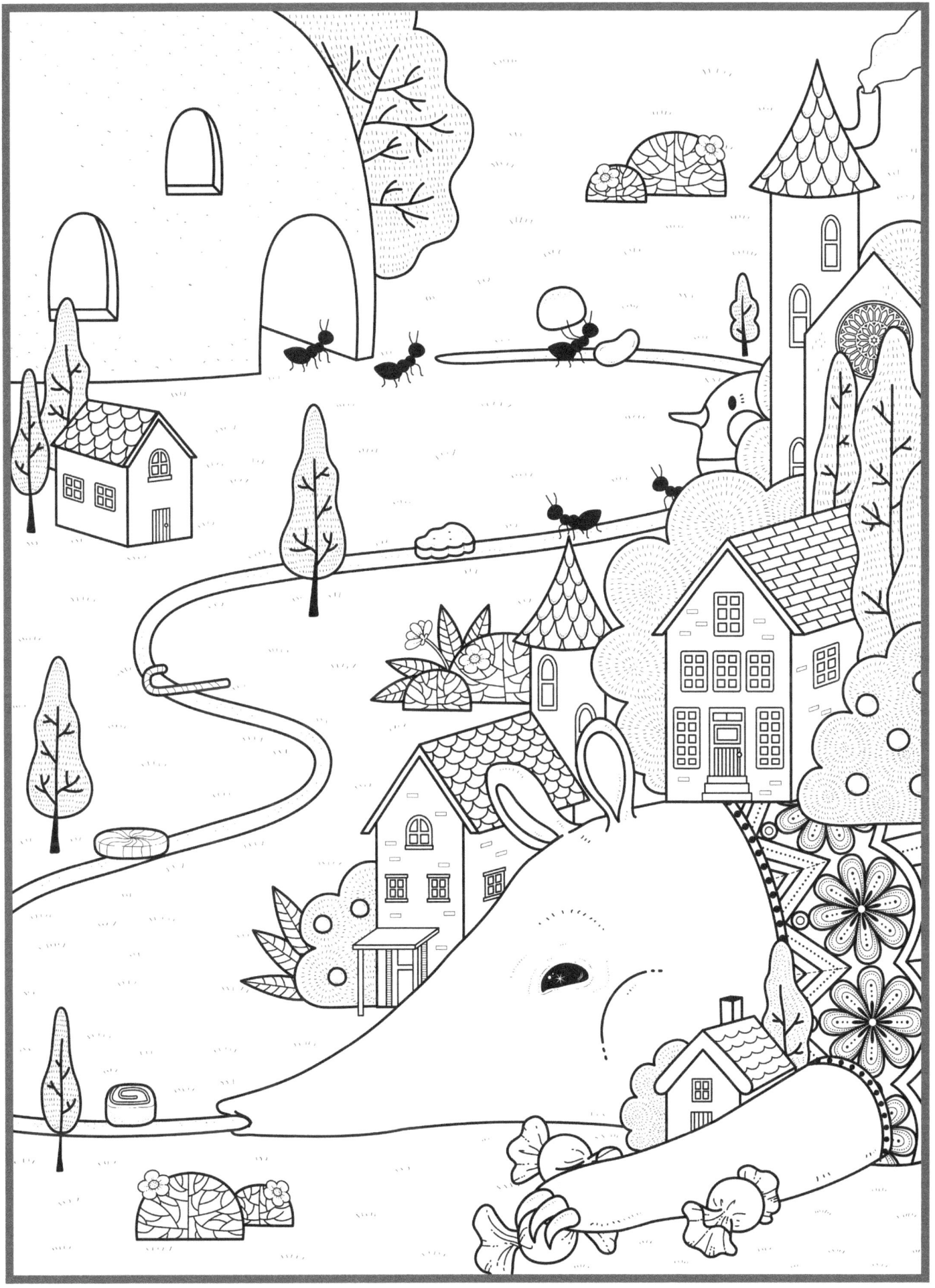

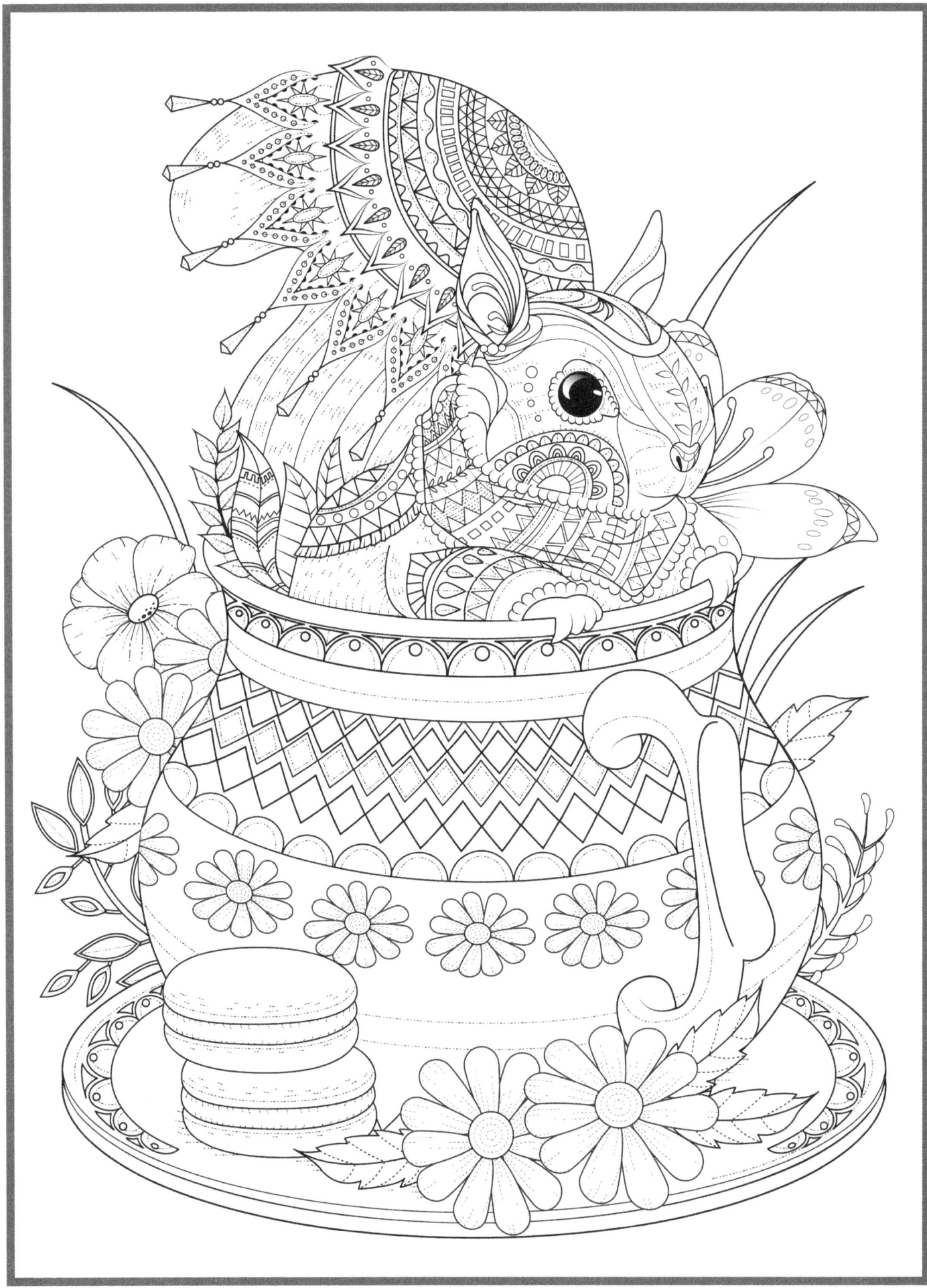

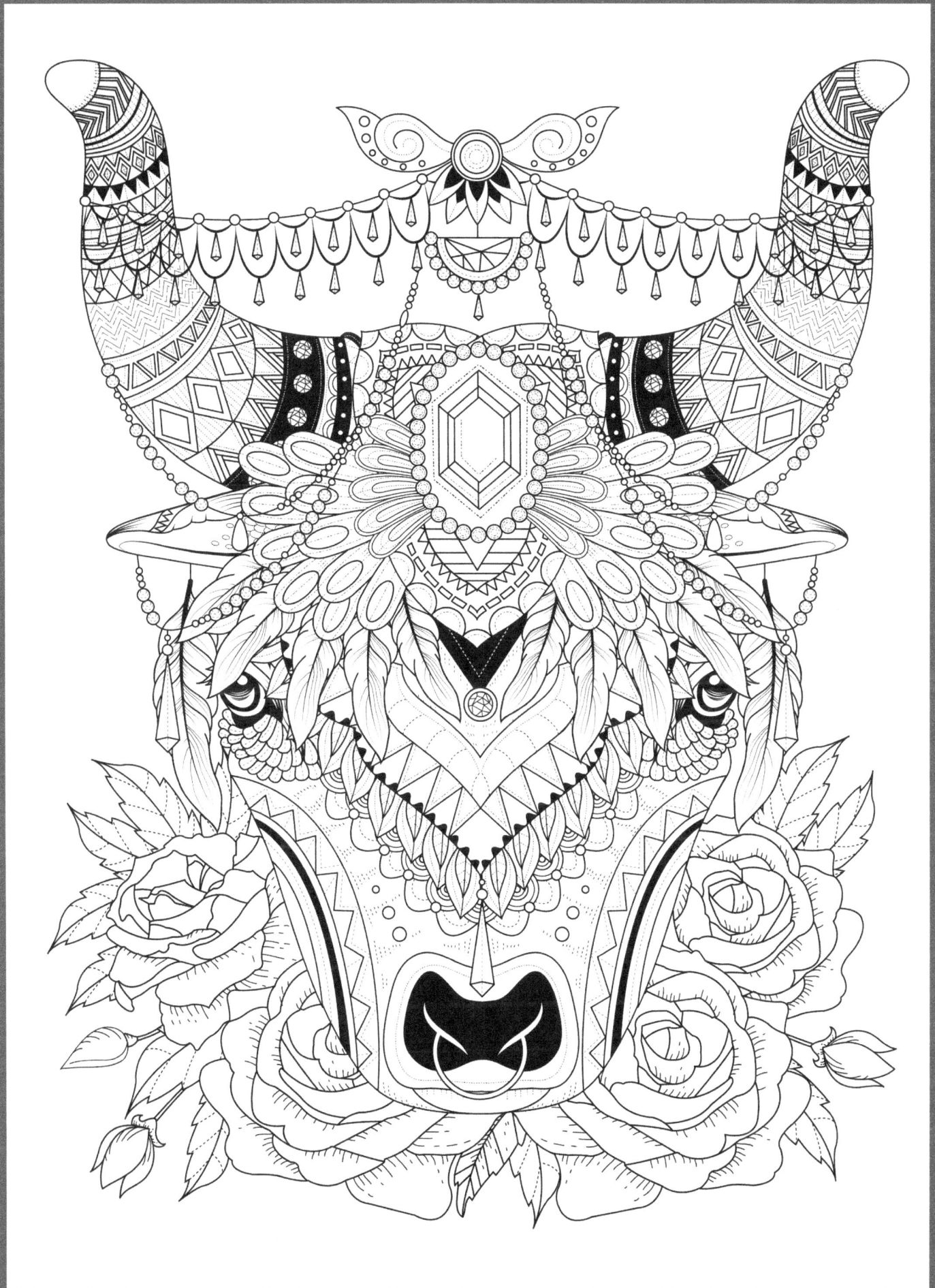

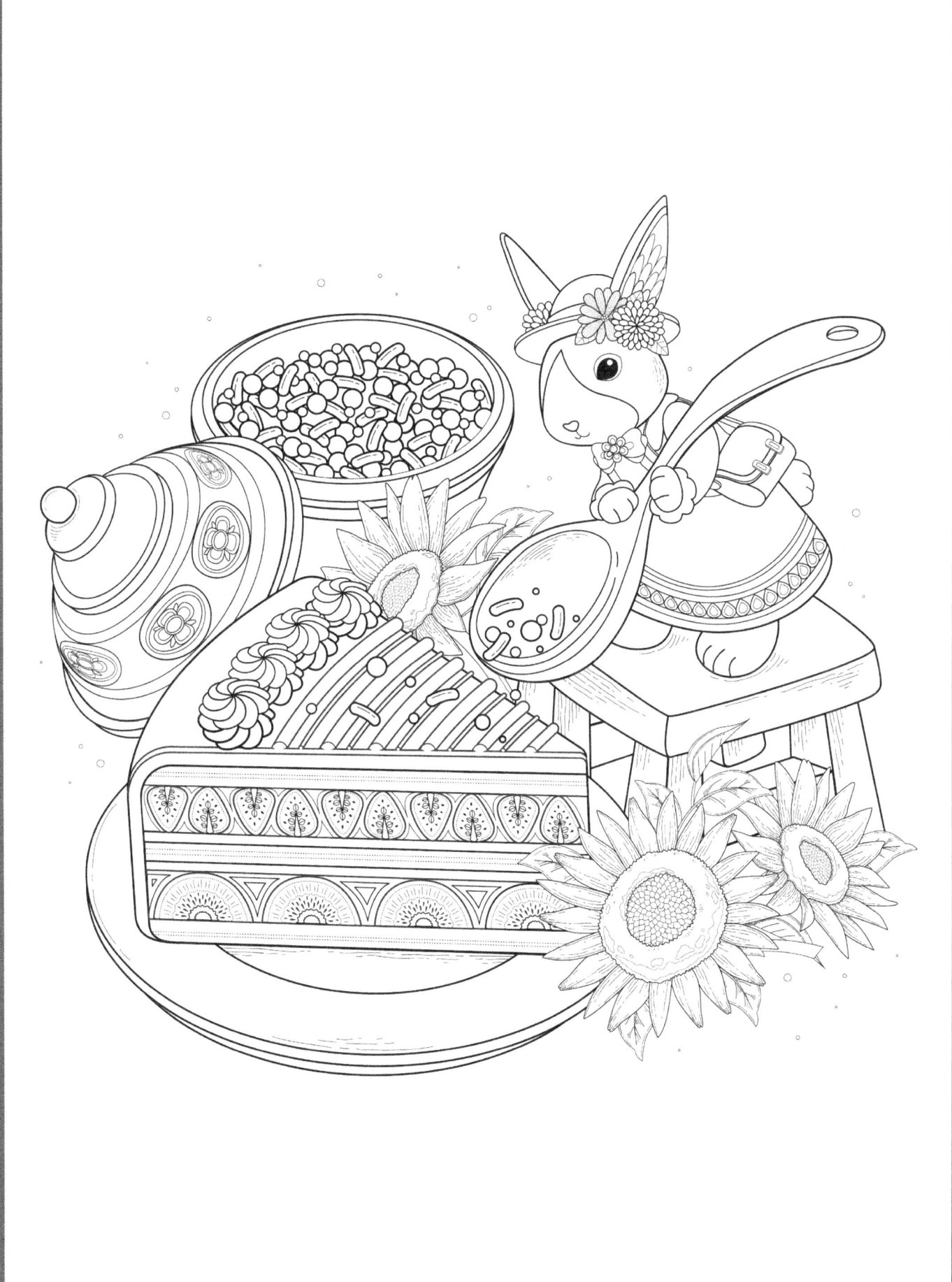

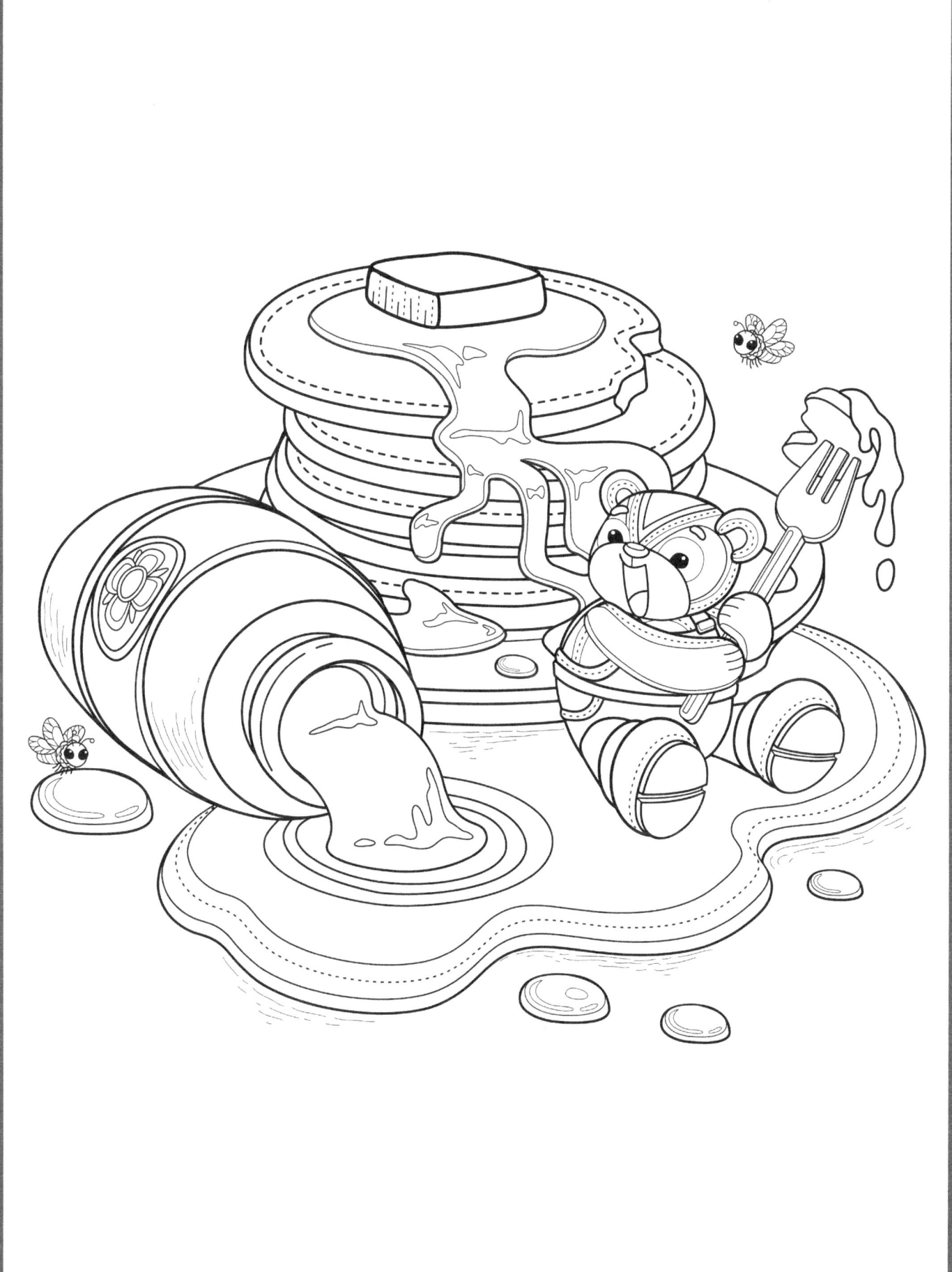

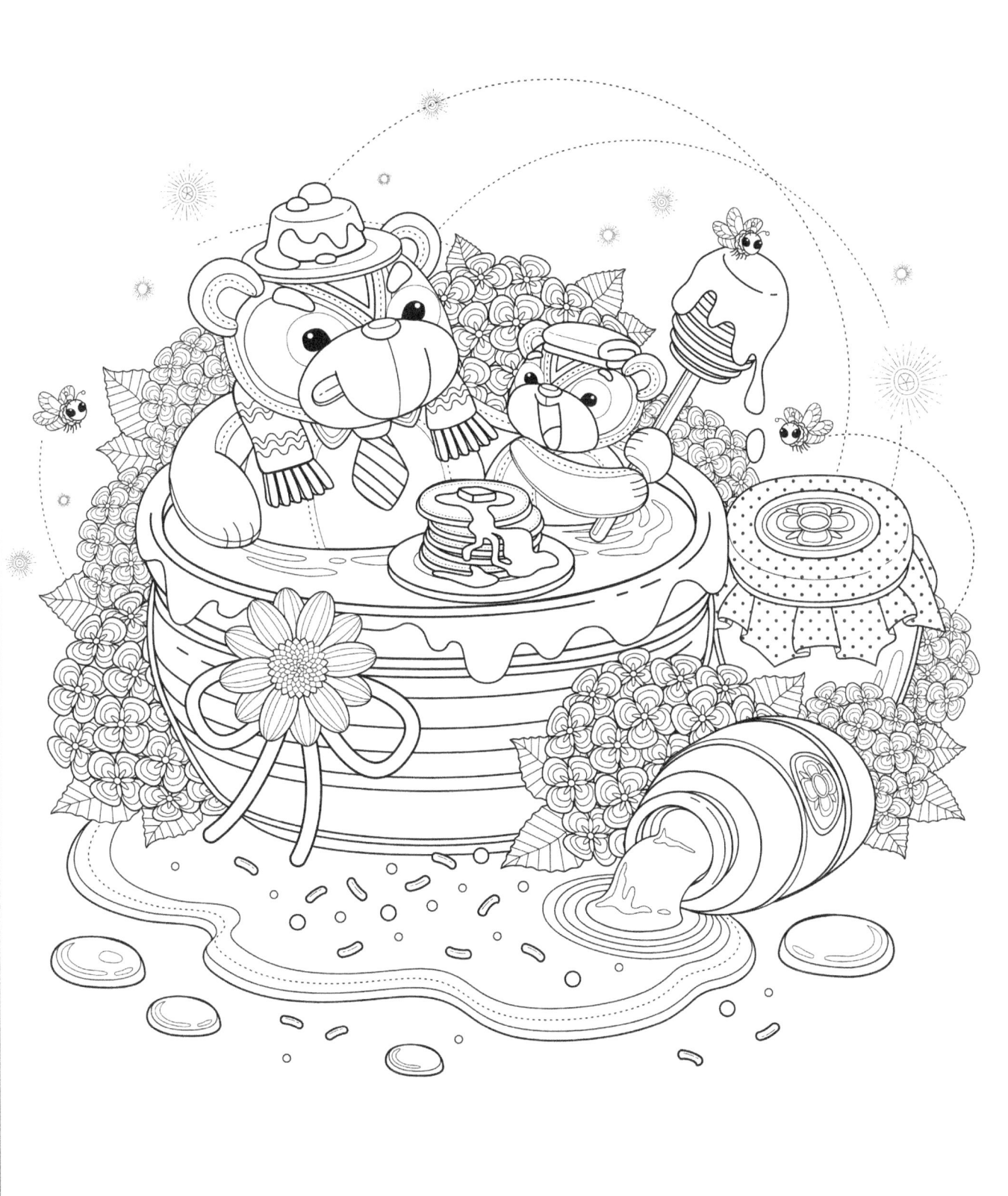

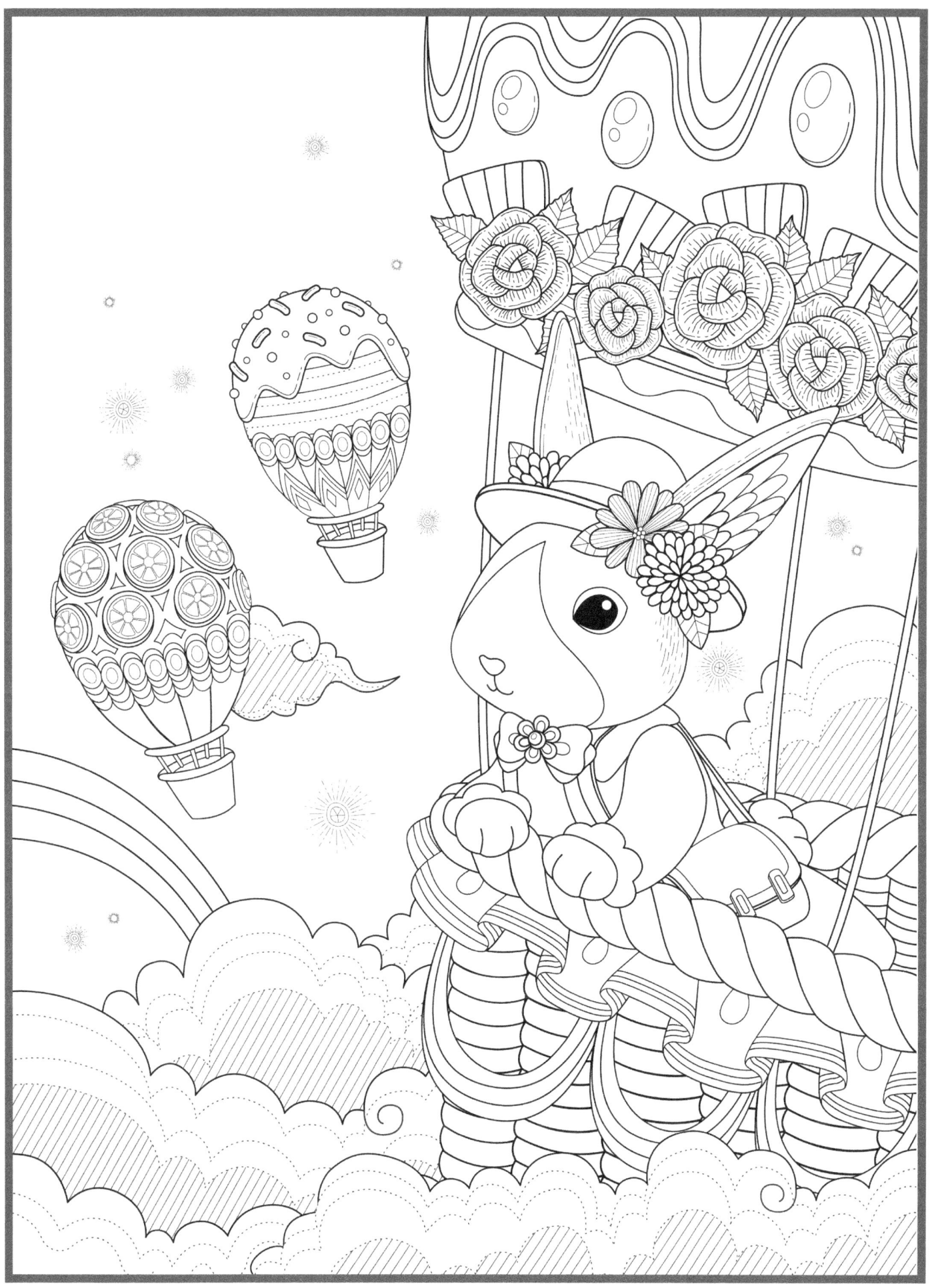

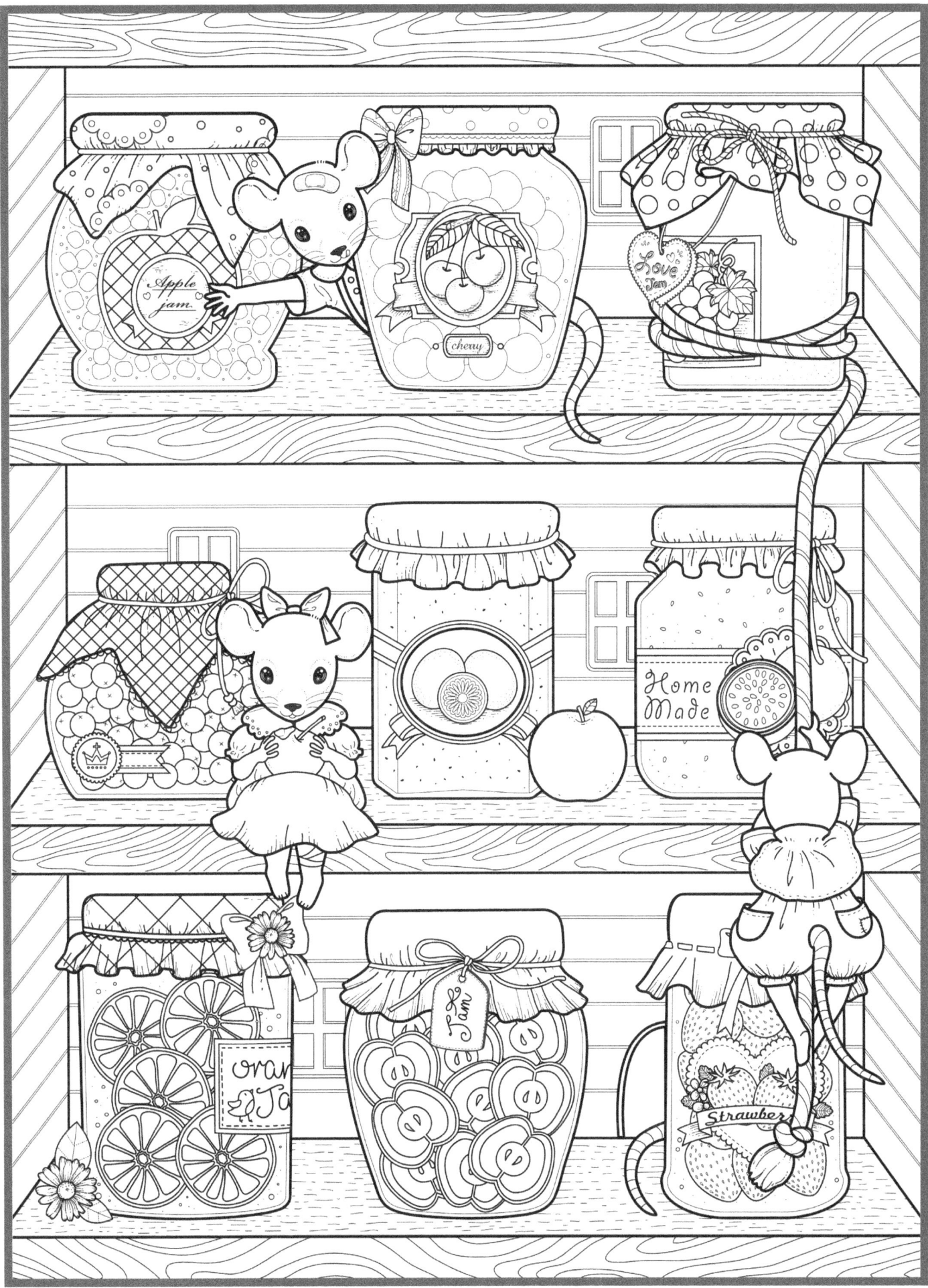

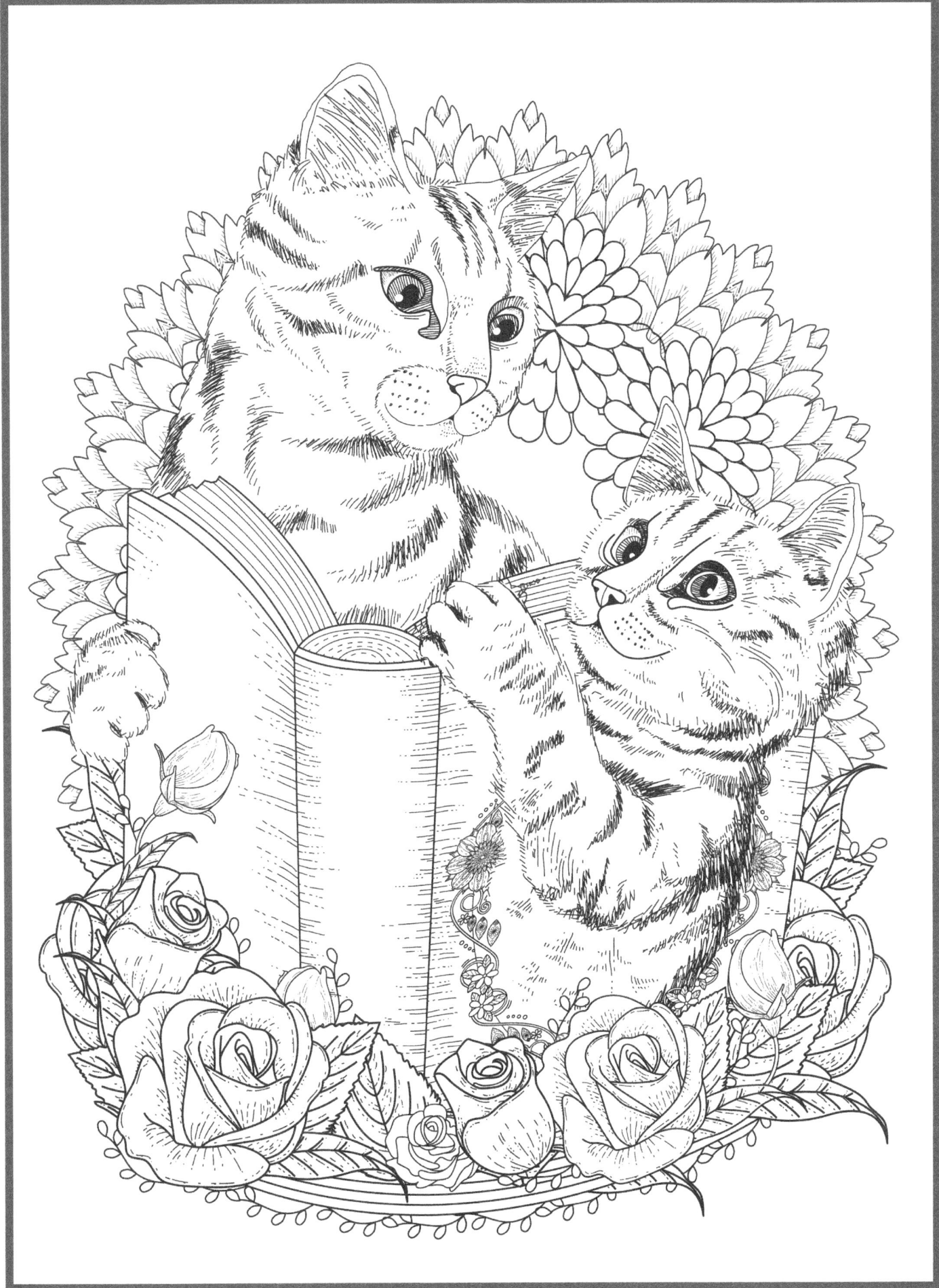

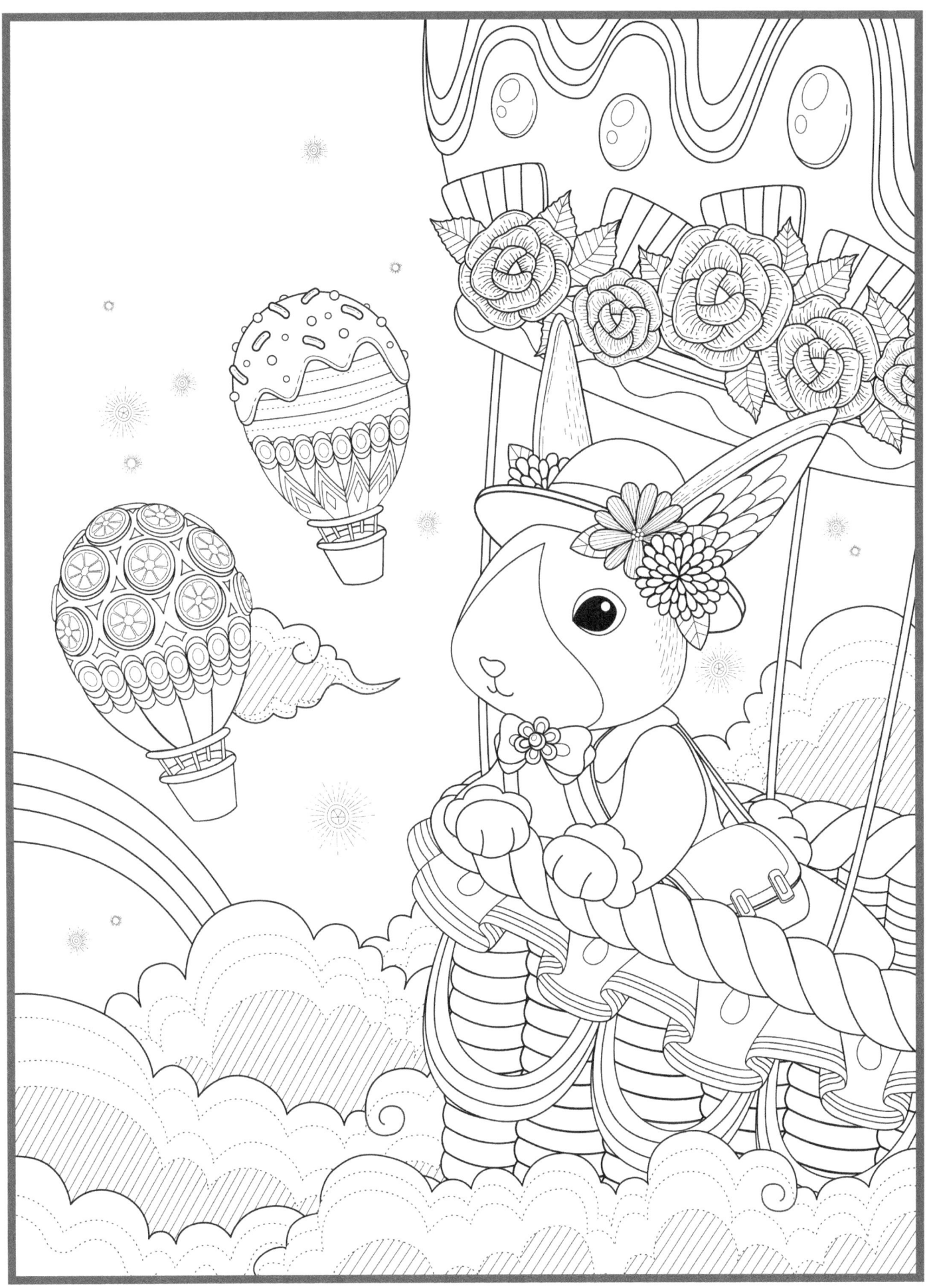

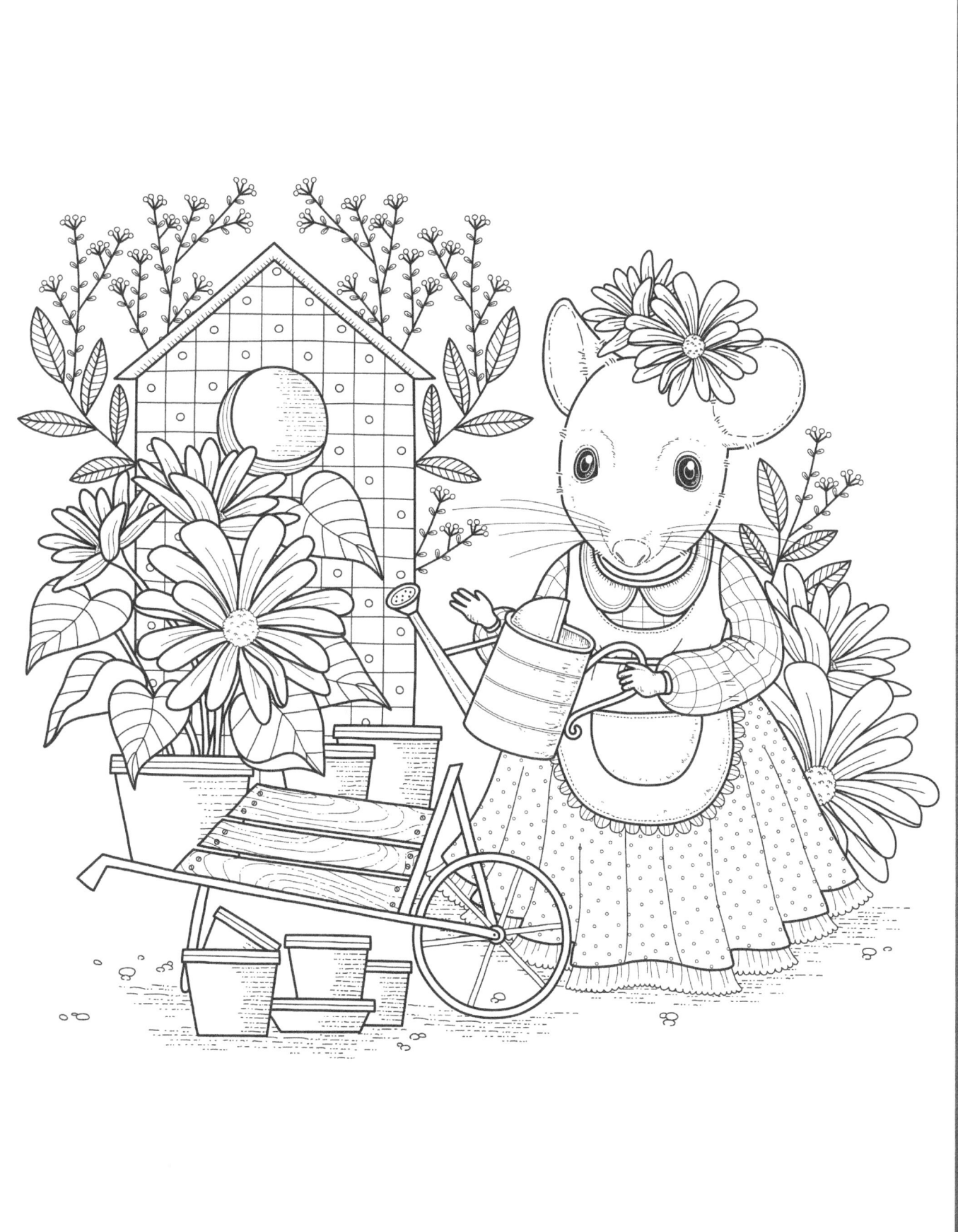

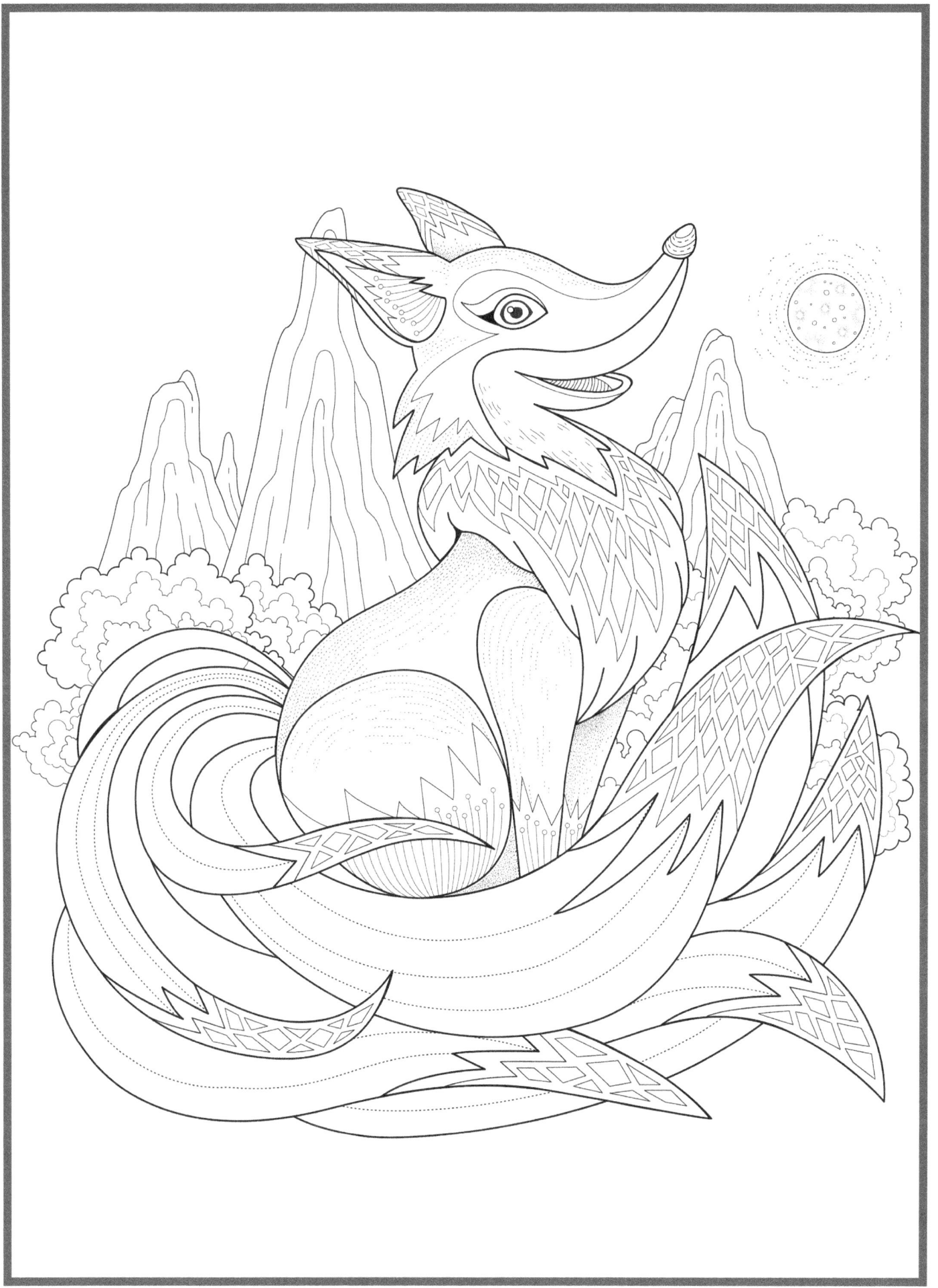

Claim your gift
SCAN ME!

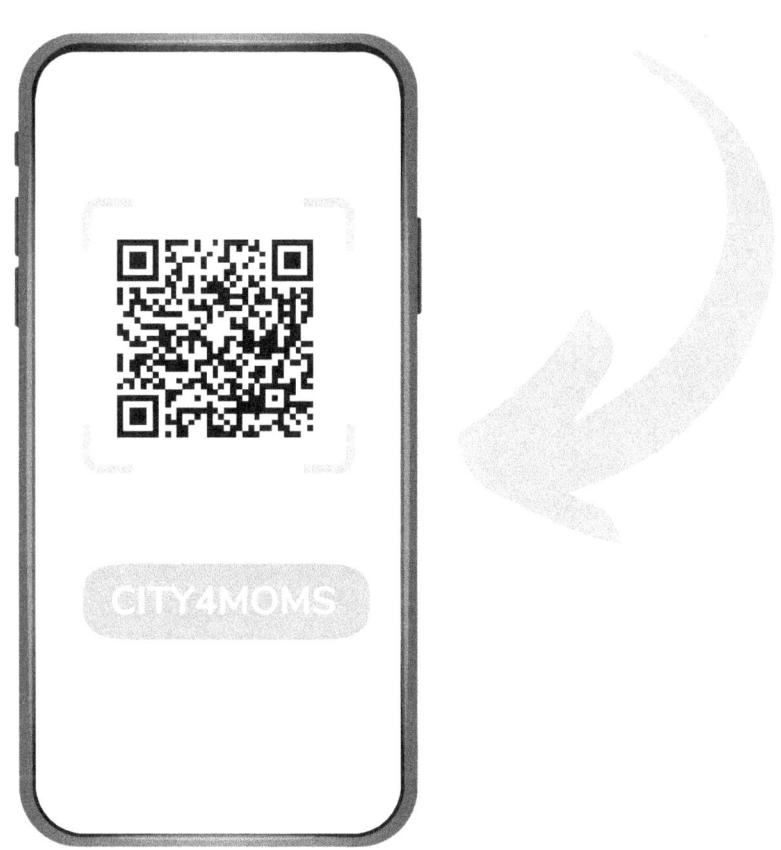

Scan the QR Code or follow the link below to find out our books and claim your free gift

https://city4moms-publishing.com/city4moms-publishing-bonus/

If you liked this coloring book and if you enjoyed it, please take a little time to review it on Amazon.
Your honest feedback would be greatly appreciated.

www.ingramcontent.com/pod-product-compliance
Lightning Source LLC
Chambersburg PA
CBHW081058240526

45465CB00025B/2711